Murderous Minds

Stories of Real-Life Murderers that Escaped the Headlines

Murderous Minds Volume 1

Ryan Becker, True Crime Seven

TRUE CRIME 7

Copyright © 2020 by Sea Vision Publishing, LLC

All Rights Reserved.

No part of this publication may be reproduced, distributed, or transmitted in any form or by any means, including photocopying, recording, electronic or mechanical methods, without the prior written permission of the publisher, except in the case of brief quotations embodied in critical reviews and certain other non-commercial uses permitted by copyright law.

Much research, from a variety of sources, has gone into the compilation of this material. We strive to keep the information up-to-date to the best knowledge of the author and publisher; the materials contained herein is factually correct. Neither the publisher nor author will be held responsible for any inaccuracies.

ISBN: 978-1718876569

Table of Contents

Table of Contents *5*

Introduction *13*

I: Michael David Clagett *17*

    Power Play 19

    Terminated 20

    Giving in 21

    The Witchduck Assault 23

    Apprehended 28

II: Aaron Alexis *32*

    His Devil Within 33

    Fallen Between the Cracks 35

    ELF 37

    Washington Naval Yard Attack 38

III: Larry Gene Ashbrook *45*

His Private Hell 46

Wedgwood Baptist 48

IV: Sante Kimes *51*

Street Child 52

Criminal Union 53

Illegally Obsessed 55

Killer Duo 59

Silverman Murder 63

Capture 69

Convictions and Melodrama 71

V: Robert James Acremant *75*

An Unlikely Killer 77

Ecstasy 78

Desperation 80

Murder in Medford 83

One Last Time 87

VI: Josephine Victoria Gray *90*

    A Killer Lifestyle 91

    The First Husband 92

    The Second Husband 96

    The Boyfriend 100

    Changing Tactics 103

Conclusion *106*

Acknowledgments *109*

About True Crime Seven *125*

Explore the Stories of
The Murderous Minds

A Note

From True Crime Seven

Hi there!

Thank you so much for picking up our book! Before you continue your exploration into the dark world of killers, we wanted to take a quick moment to explain the purpose of our books.

Our goal is to simply explore and tell the stories of various killers in the world: from unknown murderers to infamous serial killers. Our books are designed to be short and inclusive; we want to tell a good scary true story that anyone can enjoy regardless of their reading level.

That is why you won't see too many fancy words or complicated sentence structures in our books. Also, to prevent the typical cut and dry style of true crime books, we try to keep the narrative easy to follow while incorporating fiction style storytelling. As to information, we often find ourselves with too little or too much. So, in terms of research material and content, we always try to include what further helps the story of the killer.

Lastly, we want to acknowledge that, much like history, true crime is a subject that can often be interpreted differently. Depending on the topic and your upbringing, you might agree or disagree with how we present a story. We understand disagreements are inevitable. That is why we added this note so hopefully, it can help you better understand our position and goal.

Now without further ado, let the exploration to the dark begin!

Introduction

IN THIS FIRST VOLUME OF *MURDEROUS MINDS: Stories of Real-Life Murderers That Escaped The Headlines*, you will dive into the dark lives of individuals who committed gruesome killings to achieve their ends. The six killers profiled in this book will provide you with a revealing look into their gruesome crimes and their distorted thinking. In this volume, you will read about:

- Michael David Clagett, who carried out a bloody massacre at Virginia Beach's Witchduck's Inn. He was so unhinged he even murdered those who had helped him in the past. His killings were the result of his domineering girlfriend losing her job there.

- Aaron Alexis, the former naval officer who went on a shooting spree at the Washington Naval Yard. The combination of a troubled past and security failures led to this mass shooting.
- Larry Gene Ashbrook, whose delusional thinking led him to shoot up a youth event at the Wedgwood Baptist Church. At the beginning of the shooting, some people thought he was part of a skit!
- Sante Kimes, a sixty-five-year-old mother who carried out a crime spree with her adult son. Their crimes were so outrageous they became known as "Mommy and Clyde." Despite the fact she had plenty of money, her insatiable greed led to a string of murders.
- Robert James Acremant, with a military background, an MBA, and his own company, killed three people over money so he could win the attention of a stripper.
- Josephine Victoria Gray, a fifty-five-year-old grandmother who murdered two husbands and one boyfriend to collect insurance money. She used voodoo against her victims and prosecutors.

Murderous Minds provides background information of each killer, details of their crimes, and the aftermath of their deadly actions. When possible, you will get insight into each killer's mind, their deadly mind. Get ready to delve into the dark side!

I
Michael David Clagett

MICHAEL D. CLAGETT SAW THE PRISON GUARDS approaching his cell. It was time.

One guard unlocked the cell door, and two other guards secured him in handcuffs and leg shackles. Clagett exchanged a few words with them as they started walking in silence toward the room of the corrections center where his execution would take place.

For Clagett, the brief walk down the cold, sterile hallways of the Greensville Correction Center seemed to take forever. It was not because he dreaded what awaited him. On the contrary, Clagett welcomed his execution.

He was offered two options for his execution; lethal injection or the electric chair. He chose the electric chair. He thought it was ironic. He felt he deserved to die; yet, around twenty people had gathered outside the prison to hold a candlelight vigil. The gathering was organized by Virginians for Alternatives to the Death Penalty. They sang songs and read passages from the Bible.

The thirty-nine-year-old Clagett would be the second inmate executed by electric chair since the state of Virginia passed a law offering inmates a choice. He had been on death row for six years and was serving five death sentences, one for each person he had killed on June 30, 1994.

His trial ended with the jury convicting him of four counts of capital murder in the commission of a robbery, along with one count of multiple homicide murder.

As the guards led him into the room where his execution would take place, he saw a small group of people, some family members of his victims, seated in the viewing room. They would witness his execution. Some were standing. Two of those standing were his mother and his wife Karen, who he had married while on death row. Both were in tears. Though he fully accepted his fate, he would die with unanswered questions; why did he do it? Why did he allow his girlfriend, Denise, talk him into killing those people?

Power Play

Denise Holsinger separated from her husband, Randell Holsinger, in 1993, and met Clagett soon after. Clagett was everything her husband was not. While her husband was a first-class petty officer in the Navy, Clagett was chronically unemployed, had a history of committing domestic violence, and a long history of drinking and using drugs. She had her own demons and engaged in drinking and drug use. She had three children, whom she left with her husband as she did not feel she could deal with the responsibility. She just wanted out, and Clagett appealed to her because of his wild streak. She'd grown tired of being the proper Navy wife. Clagett's irresponsible manner provided the freedom to express her discontent with life.

Holsinger met Clagett at her place of work, the Witchduck Inn. Located on Pembroke Boulevard, in Virginia Beach, Witchduck Inn is a tavern and restaurant, and Clagett was a regular there. Clagett frequented the tavern so often that he considered the bar owner, Lam Van Son, a friend. Son had fled his native South

Vietnam during the communist takeover. He had fought with U.S. soldiers, as he was part of South Vietnam's Special Forces unit.

When South Vietnam fell to the communist in 1975, Son was placed in a re-education camp. Son escaped the camp and traveled to Thailand by boat before coming to America. He had settled in Lynchburg, where he married Lanna Le Son in 1988.

Holsinger rented a small apartment, and Clagett moved in with her. He spent most of the time lying around the house getting stoned. Holsinger would join him when she arrived home from work. While Clagett did not contribute to the household, Holsinger allowed it.

It put her in a position where she felt she held power in the relationship, and that power came without resistance. In her marriage, she felt she had to play the role of the dutiful wife; it was different with Clagett. In their relationship, she was the one with the job and the money, and she was the one who offered him female attention.

Terminated

It was in June of 1994, the demons within Holsinger and Clagett collided to create an explosion of violence that sent the community into shock. Holsinger had been pocketing money from her job at the Witchduck Inn. She had been doing it for months; to help support the drug habit that had begun to consume both her and Clagett.

Unfortunately for Holsinger, her stealing caught up with her. Her boss, Lam Van Son, caught on to what she was doing and fired her June 28. Holsinger was livid when Son told her that he was letting her go. Instead of being grateful that Son was not going to report her crime to the police, Holsinger cursed him and blamed him for being paranoid about the whole thing. She insisted she was innocent.

Giving in

Holsinger arrived home after work to find Clagett in the living room, inhaling from a bong. He also had a bottle of whiskey. Holsinger grabbed the bong and took a few puffs before drinking from the bottle. She told Clagett about being fired as the drugs and alcohol took effect. Clagett reached out to comfort her but she pushed him away. She was determined she was going to make Son pay.

Clagett got up from the couch and took her in his arms, telling her it would be all right; somehow, they would make it. Clagett's attempts to console her were not working; he could see that she remained upset. He thought he knew what would help. He ran his drunk, stoned hands all over her before pulling her into the bedroom. They had wild and intense sex; the kind he knew would get her to release the pressure she kept inside.

The next morning, as the two of them lay in bed, Holsinger divulged her plan. She wanted Clagett with her when she robbed the Witchduck. She stroked his chest and told him after they got the money, they could get away and find a new place to live.

She had ideas of going to Mexico or Canada. Clagett seemed hesitant in agreeing to her plan. The worst offense he was ever jailed for was committing domestic violence against his last two wives. Because of the brutality of his crimes, he had been jailed for several years. Still, he wanted to please Holsinger. She convinced him by comparing them to Bonnie and Clyde. They would be free and famous.

He wanted Holsinger's approval. It led him to agree. In his mind, Clagett had nothing to lose and everything to gain. For the next two days, the couple would binge on drugs and alcohol.

The Witchduck Assault

On June 30, thirty-one-year-old Karen Rounds arrived for her shift at the Witchduck Inn. She had been hired by Son to replace Holsinger as their new waitress. A Pennsylvania native, Rounds moved to Virginia Beach with her husband, Kevin Rounds.

Rounds had been a nurse but looking for a career change. She had worked as a nurse at a state prison while her husband was in the Navy. When they moved to Virginia Beach, she got a job working at the Maryview Medical Center; a clinic located in Churchland. She quit her job to go back to school to study computers.

Her new job at the Witchduck Inn would provide her with some spending money while attending classes. Both Karen and her husband knew Clagett as they often saw him when they went to Witchduck. Karen found Clagett to be creepy, but her husband had reassured her that he would not harm anyone.

When she entered the Witchduck Inn, she was greeted by Abdelaziz Gren, one of the regulars. Gren was born in Morocco and came to the United States so he could live the American Dream, which included owning his own business and having his own home and car. He had learned English and attended college while living in Morocco so that he would be prepared when he arrived in the 'promised land.' He spoke fluent Arabic, English, and French. Upon arriving in America, Gren attended Old Dominion University, while working in his family's restaurant.

Everyone who knew him spoke of his big heart and how he would help anybody in need. During Thanksgiving, Gren had been taking a walk along the Lynnhaven River, where he came across a fisherman. The fisherman was taking fish below the size limit. Gren brought this to the attention of the man, who replied that he depended on his catch to feed his family.

Gren went to a local grocery store and bought food for the man and his family. He once told his sister that his altruism came from his gratitude for all the opportunities he had received since coming to this country. Gren frequently gave Clagett money so he could buy food, and would occasionally treat him to drinks at the Witchduck.

Rounds entered the kitchen where she saw Son talking to Wendel Parrish. Parrish was the tavern's cook and handyman. He was born in Prince George, Virginia, and later moved to Hampton Roads. He attended Bayside High School, where he graduated in

1981. The thirty-two-year-old Parrish would often treat Clagett to meals at the tavern.

Rounds was busy that day as the Witchduck attracted a larger crowd than normal as Son had the World Cup on the tavern's big-screen television. Later that night, the crowd emptied into the street. There were only a few patrons left, one of which was Gren. Rounds walked through the rear exit of the tavern and into the humid night air to take a break. What she did not realize was that it would be the last work break she would ever take.

When Rounds finished her break, she stepped back inside and returned to the kitchen. She saw Son and Parrish working. Right off the kitchen was a small room where Son's five-year-old son, Joshua, was sleeping. Son frequently brought Joshua to work as his wife worked.

She went back to the dining area to check on her customers when she spotted Clagett and Holsinger. Holsinger was playing pool while Clagett was at a nearby table.

Seeing Holsinger and Clagett made her uncomfortable. She had a bad feeling about Clagett. Now that Holsinger had been fired, she did not trust her, either. Little did Rounds know, she was minutes away from Virginia Beach's first quadruple murder.

As per Holsinger's plan, Clagett monitored the activity in the small tavern as Holsinger played pool. Holsinger looked at Clagett, waiting for him to make eye contact with her; their mutual eye contact was the signal to make their move. The audience for the World Cup had left along with most of the regulars. The remaining people in the tavern were Son, Parrish, Rounds, and Gren.

Holsinger gave Clagett a nod and rushed to the counter, jumping over it. She went straight for the cash register as Clagett pulled out a .357-Magnum revolver and joined her behind the counter. He ordered everyone in the restaurant to gather in the kitchen and get on the floor.

Everyone but Parrish complied. He refused to give in to the threats and remained on his barstool. Holsinger tried to get Clagett to 'do it!' Clagett hesitated. Holsinger was insistent that he comply. She repeated her order. Clagett collected his nerve, placed the barrel of his gun inches from Parrish's face and pulled the trigger.

The bullet passed through Parrish's head, and he slumped forward on the bar. Rounds screamed in terror as she lay on the floor. Son and Gren remained silent and did not move. Holsinger ordered Clagett to continue shooting the rest of them. One by one, Clagett shot each person on the floor execution-style, placing his gun to the back of their head and shooting. When he was done, the kitchen floor was covered in blood.

Holsinger grabbed four hundred dollars from the register. A small pittance for their efforts. When they were about to take off, Holsinger noticed Son's son, Joshua, sleeping in the other room. Holsinger ordered Clagett to shoot the child. Telling him they could not leave any witnesses.

Clagett could not pull the trigger on the sleeping child. Fearful of waiting for a second longer, Holsinger fled without Clagett. She drove off in their car, leaving Clagett behind. Still strung out from the drugs and alcohol from the previous two days, Clagett felt a deep sense of fear as he stared at the bloody, dead bodies. He screamed and ran out of the tavern into the dark, humid night.

At midnight, one of the regulars, Richard T. Reed, arrived at the Witchduck Inn for a drink. The Witchduck was open until two in the morning; however, Reed found the front door locked. He heard music playing inside, so he went around to the back entrance. To his surprise, the rear entrance was unlocked. Normally, the back door was locked.

Upon entering the tavern, he was met with a very bloody scene: bloodied bodies on the kitchen floor and Parrish slumped over the bar.

He called 911 and was soon joined by another regular, who was well-liked by Joshua. Joshua called the man "Uncle Richie." Knowing Joshua frequently slept at the restaurant, he ran inside.

With a singular focus, the man made his way past the dead bodies, over the blood-covered floor, and reached the room. To his relief, Joshua was unharmed but terrified. The man comforted Joshua and carried him out of the restaurant, making sure to cover his eyes.

Minutes later, Joshua was sitting in the back seat of a squad car with "Uncle Richie," who was comforting him. Both of them watched as bodies, covered by blankets, were pushed by on gurneys as first responders loaded them into the back of the waiting ambulances.

Apprehended

On July 1, 1994, Virginia Beach Police Officer Donna Malcolm was on patrol when she received a call requesting an officer respond to a disturbance. When she arrived at the address, the resident told Malcolm that a man was sleeping in the bushes of her front yard.

Malcolm arrested the man for public intoxication and brought him to police headquarters, where he was questioned by Detective Yoakum. The man Yoakum was interviewing was Clagett.

What Clagett did not know was that police had arrested Holsinger earlier. She had been pulled over for reckless driving when she had fled the crime scene. Because Holsinger provided a description of Clagett, Yoakum had a strong suspicion that the man he was talking to was the murderer; however, Clagett continued to deny any involvement with the Witchduck Inn killings.

Yoakum deceived Clagett, by telling him he had been caught by the tavern's security cameras at the time of the murders. Hearing this, Clagett stopped denying his involvement and confessed to the killings.

The police detective told Clagett that was exactly what they would be asking the court. His rant during confession: 'Fry me; I'm not gonna live. I don't want the taxpayers supporting me. I did it. Yeah, I did it. I did it all. All-by-my-fucking-self. Let that little cunt go free. I did it all. I did it all buddy. And the worst thing was Lam (Son) was my buddy!'

Later that same day, a reporter from WTKR Channel 3 news asked Clagett if he was guilty of the charges. Clagett replied to the reporter, 'Yes. I shot every one of them.'

Clagett later reversed himself by claiming that his confessions of guilt were made while he was still under the influence of drugs. He was put on trial. The ten-day trial ended with the jury finding Clagett guilty of four counts of capital murder, one count of multiple homicide capital murder, robbery, and the use of a firearm.

On October 24, 1995, Clagett was placed on death row.

A year later, Clagett married his first cousin, Karen Elaine Sparks, in a jailhouse ceremony.

On July 6, 2000, Clagett was strapped to the electric chair while some family members of the victims, Clagett's mother, and his new wife, looked on in silence. Clagett was expressionless at first, then broke down while he apologized to the victim's families.

Once he was secured in the chair, the first of two electrical charges were discharged. The first charge was eighteen hundred twenty-five volts and lasted thirty seconds, while the second charge was two hundred and forty volts for sixty seconds. He was pronounced dead after the second shock.

He would be the last person in the United States to be executed using the electric chair.

Holsinger is serving five life sentences plus twenty-three years in the Fluvanna Correctional Center for Women.

II

Aaron Alexis

IT WAS THE MORNING OF AUGUST 16, 2013, WHEN Aaron Alexis drove away from the Residence Inn Hotel in his rental car and headed for a Washington naval yard. He arrived in Southwest Washington, D.C., on August 25.

He had stayed at a few hotels before selecting the Residence Inn. Alexis had never been a good sleeper. Plagued by insomnia, every night was a battle for him.

September 16, 2013, Aaron Alexis was on a mission, and he would execute that mission at the headquarters of the Naval Sea Systems Command (NAVSEA) in the Washington naval yard.

His duffel bag contained a Remington 870 Express 12-gauge shotgun; purchased two days earlier. It had been disassembled so it could be concealed in the duffel bag.

For Aaron Alexis, the day would reach a threshold. His had been a life of beating the odds while being beaten by his own demons. A life full of contradictions. He was a practitioner of Buddhism; while having a long history of gun offenses. He was among the rescuers during the September 11 attack.

His life had not always been like this, but by the time September 16, 2013 rolled around, his evil intentions had consumed him, and he was going to make others pay.

His Devil Within

Aaron Alexis was born May 9, 1979, in the boroughs of Queens, New York City. Alexis was a reflection of the racial diversity that existed there. An African American, Alexis embraced the Asian culture, in particular, Thai culture.

Later, when he moved to Fort Worth, Texas, Alexis immersed himself in Thai society. He studied Thai language and was a regular at Buddhist temples, where he chanted and meditated. He also became a waiter in a Thai restaurant, owned by friends of his. He worked there for free so that he could further immerse himself in their culture.

In 2007, he became a Navy reservist, where he was a full-time aviation electrician's mate. He advanced to the rank of petty officer third class but left the reserves in 2011 on a general discharge as he wanted to go back to school. He took online courses at Embry-Riddle Aeronautical University, where he studied aeronautics while working as a civilian contractor at the Fleet Logistics Support Squadron 46.

In 2013, Alexis started going to the Veterans Administration to seek treatment for insomnia. He was prescribed trazodone for depression and insomnia. However, the medication was not enough as he also suffered from paranoia and heard voices. Just two weeks before his visit to the Veterans Administration, he had called the police to report that people were talking to him through the walls and ceiling of his hotel room. He also told them that people were transmitting microwave vibrations into his body to prevent him from getting sleep.

His mental issues had caused him plenty of trouble in the past, but he always managed to skate by. In 2004, when he was living in Seattle at his grandmother's home, Alexis fired three rounds from his .45-caliber pistol at a construction worker's car. He had been frustrated with the parking situation the work site caused him. When he was questioned by police, he told them he could not remember the incident, and that he also experienced post-traumatic stress from the time he had been involved with the rescue attempts after the September 11 attack.

Alexis was arrested for the incident but was never charged, as was the case in a 2010 incident. In that situation, he had discharged a gun in his Fort Worth apartment. A neighbor, who occupied a second-floor unit in the same building, called police to report gunfire had entered through her floor, nearly hitting her. Alexis lived in the apartment below. She felt that it was his way of getting back at her for an earlier confrontation. When questioned by police, he told them that his gun had accidentally fired while he was cleaning it. He was arrested, but the charges were later dismissed.

Fallen Between the Cracks

When Aaron Alexis's commander found out about the arrest, he had his legal officer write up a memo recommending Alexis's removal from the navy. That memo was shelved after his commander decided not to pursue charges against him. Alexis, once again, escaped punishment for his reckless ways.

The Remington 870 Express 12-gauge shotgun concealed in the bag on his passenger seat was not his first choice of weapon. Alexis had easily purchased it at Sharpshooter's Small Arms Range, located in Lorton, Virginia, only 15 miles from the south of Washington. While there, he had test-fired an AR-15 semi-automatic rifle but decided to go with a handgun instead.

There was a problem with getting the handgun. Virginia law makes it illegal to sell handguns to individuals who live out of state. If he wanted the handgun, it would have to be shipped to a gun shop in his state. It was because of this technicality he decided to go with the Remington 870. He also purchased twenty-four rounds of ammunition. Because he had never been charged with the two previous shooting incidents, he passed the state and federal background checks.

Alexis was upset with the navy because he felt he had been cheated out of pay. He had worked for three months in Japan on the Navy's intranet network while employed at Experts Inc., a contractor of Hewlett-Packard, which provides support to the navy.

ELF

He returned to stateside in January of 2013, but felt he had not been properly compensated. He believed he was being discriminated against. However, Alexis had other concerns about the navy.

He was a member of an online chat room that catered to those who believed mind control was being used on the public. The group Freedom from Covert Harassment & Surveillance believed that the navy was using extremely low-frequency waves (ELF) to target brains.

In one online message to the group, Alexis stated, 'My name is Aaron. I am ex-navy. I fear the consistent bombardment from the ELF weapon is starting to take its toll on my body.'

While he was on a naval assignment in Newport, RI, he changed hotel rooms three times out of the belief that people were sending messages of persuasion through the microwave oven in his room. Alexis believed the navy was using ELF on the American public and that he was one of its victims. He saw it as his mission to take revenge on those who were perpetrating this crime. He even etched into the stock of his shotgun, 'my ELF Weapon.'

Washington Naval Yard Attack

Alexis reached the security gate at the Washington Naval Yard at twenty minutes after eight in the morning. He had no problem entering as he had secret-level security clearance and a common access card (C.A.C); standard military identification card. That Alexis was able to obtain the proper security credentials was just another example of Alexis managing to beat the system.

When he had enlisted in June 2007, he never mentioned the Seattle incident when filling out the questionnaire. The questionnaire required applicants to indicate if they have ever been arrested. Though his arrest showed up during a fingerprint check by the FBI, it was never followed-up on. Even though he had been out of the navy reserves for a whole year, his clearance was good for ten years, and he was working for the navy as a contractor.

It would appear that whenever Alexis got into trouble, he managed to escape prosecution because someone in the process dropped the ball. The nation would, in a few hours, learn about the ramifications of this and its horrific nature.

Having passed security, Alexis drove to Building 197, an eleven-story structure where three thousand people reported to work. He got out of the car and walked to the entrance with the duffle bag over his shoulder. The building was beginning to fill up with people arriving for work.

Alexis calmly got in an elevator and took it to the fourth floor. He was relieved that he was the only one in it. The fewer people who noticed him, the better. When he reached the fourth floor, he walked briskly to the men's room, passing numerous people along the way. He felt a great sense of relief upon discovering the bathroom empty. He took out the shotgun from the duffel bag and began reassembling it. He feared someone might enter the restroom and catch him in the act. But this was not the case. He successfully reassembled his shotgun and loaded it. Armed, he stepped out of the bathroom and immediately began shooting.

Thirty-nine-year-old Bertillia Lavern was working on the fourth floor in one of the offices when she heard a loud but muffled bang. She knew that one of the departments was holding an event and assumed that someone had dropped a folding table. When the banging sounds continued, she knew instinctively what was happening.

As a navy medical specialist, and having trained with the Marines, she was very familiar with the sound of gunfire. She dropped to the ground as did her supervisor, Andy Kelly. They crawled under a desk and waited silently as the shots continued. At one point, Lavern heard glass shattering above her head. She and Kelly feared they had been spotted by Alexis, but he never appeared.

Alexis was indiscriminate in his shooting; he shot at anyone in his sight. The hallways and open spaces of the fourth floor were littered with broken glass and pieces of plaster from the shot-up walls. Trails of blood led to where eight people had lost their lives.

Suspended over all of this was an eerie silence as Alexis made his way toward the third floor, where he killed two additional people in their office. Leaving the office, he shot at people in the hallway but missed them. Alexis was headed for the staircase when he caught sight of a female employee hiding behind a file cabinet and metal beam. He aimed and pulled the trigger, but his gun did not fire. Frustrated, he took off and reloaded in the stairwell.

While he was reloading, he spotted a group of employees walking down the stairs. Upon seeing Alexis, they turned and ran back up the stairs. Alexis shot at them, hitting a woman in the shoulder. Rather than following them, he continued his descent down the stairs.

The group that encountered Alexis in the stairs made their way to the roof. One of them wrote a note indicating they needed medical assistance for the woman and dropped it off the roof to the street below. An MPD officer spotted the note and called emergency responders. The group was evacuated by helicopter.

Lavern and Kelly waited until they believed Alexis had moved on to escape from the building. Kelly was the first one to get up from behind the desk to determine if it was safe to leave. In doing so, he caught a glimpse of co-worker Vishnu Pandit, lying on the other side of the room. They rushed over to him to check on his condition. The sixty-one-year-old father and grandfather, who'd had a career in the navy that spanned thirty years, had been shot in the temple but had a pulse.

Lavern cradled him in her arms as she applied pressure to his wound with her hand. She felt his breath as she prayed for him. Kelly volunteered to find help while Lavern stayed behind with Pandit, telling him how much he was loved as he lay unconscious.

Half an hour later, three security guards arrived at Lavern and Pandit. They used an office chair to roll him to the staircase. From there, they used an evacuation chair, to assist disabled people in times of an emergency, to move him down the stairs. The wheels of the evacuation chair were not working, so they had to carry him down.

They made it to the second floor when an announcement came across the radio of one of the security guards, informing them that the gunman was on the west side of the first floor. When the group reached the bottom of the staircase, they exited the building using a side door. A security guard in an unmarked vehicle spotted them and picked them up. As they drove away, Lavern checked Pandit's pulse again; he was dead.

The first call made to 911 was by an employee on the fourth floor. He had made the call when he witnessed Alexis fire at his first victim; a young woman hit in the head and her hand. The caller got under his desk, positioned a filing cabinet in front of him to conceal himself. It was from this position that he made the call with his cell phone at twenty-three minutes after eight in the morning.

Washington, D.C., police arrived seven minutes later. They surrounded the building and closed down roadways and bridges in the area. Neighboring schools and the United States Senate buildings were locked down.

Alexis was headed for the lobby after shooting up the third floor. It was there he killed a security guard and proceeded to pick up the officer's 9mm-Beretta semi-automatic pistol. He continued firing, using the officer's pistol as he was running low on ammunition for his shotgun.

The first floor was a maze of hallways and offices. Alexis encountered another security guard, who was with a navy MP officer. Both of them had arrived in response to the shooting. Alexis fired at both but missed. The security guard fired back but missed as Alexis took off and disappeared in the catacomb that is the first floor.

While escaping, Alexis found himself faced with other military police officers. As before, there was a shootout without anyone getting hit. Alexis took off to the stairwell on the west side of the building, looking for a way to escape from the building.

Once there, he opened a door that led to the alleyway outside, where he spotted two men. Alexis fired at the men, using the gun he had taken from the security guard. One of the men was hit and killed, while the other fled for his life. Alexis returned inside the building as he continued to evade law enforcement. Alexis was no longer the hunter; he was the hunted.

Alexis attempted to elude law enforcement by returning to the third floor, where he hid among the cubicles. He spotted a group of

MP officers headed in his direction. Alexis shot at the officers, hitting one of them in both legs. His comrades pulled him to safety and radioed for back-up. Alexis used the opportunity to sneak from the cubicle to find another hiding spot.

Another team of officers arrived and continued to search for Alexis among the sea of cubicles, which made locating him like searching for a pin in a haystack.

Dorian DeSantis, a police officer with the District of Columbia, and U.S. Park Police officer Carl Hiott were walking down the cubicle aisle when Alexis saw them approaching. He jumped from beneath the desk and started shooting.

The shot hit Hiott, who was saved by his bulletproof vest.

DeSantis got off a shot that hit Alexis in the head, killing him instantly.

In the end, Alexis killed twelve people and injured eight.

III
Larry Gene Ashbrook

THE NEIGHBORS PEEKED THROUGH THEIR curtains, watching an agitated Larry Ashbrook pace on the street. Most of the residents of the Fort Worth neighborhood were retirees, and Ashbrook's presence always made them uneasy.

He was following his usual routine of leaving his house in the morning for one hour. As always, he carried a blue canvas bag. No one knew where he went when he left. One thing they did know, they did not want any contact with him.

They were intimidated by his sinister appearance and his violent temper. They frequently witnessed him kicking the door to his car or the door to his house. Well, it was not really his house.

The forty-seven-year-old Ashbrook lived with his eighty-five-year-old father, Jack D. Ashbrook.

Jack used to work for the railroad as a switchman. Jack's neighbors feared for his safety as Larry was always cursing, knocking him down, or assaulting him physically. Though it was upsetting to the neighbors to witness this, they never contacted Texas authorities, fearing that Larry would seek retribution against them.

His Private Hell

Larry Ashbrook returned home from his morning routine. He unlocked the front door, which still had a hole in it from where he had kicked it the previous week. He walked down the hallway, whose walls were dotted with freshly patched holes, holes created by his past outbursts. He inflicted the damage, and his elderly father did the repairs.

His life started unraveling in July of 1979. Ashbrook was with the United States Navy squadron and reported to a deployment site. That date remained vivid in his memory. He had been attending a social event when a member of his squadron approached him with an unusual question. He was wondering about a murder which Ashbrook knew nothing about. What unnerved him was the tone of voice this person had used when speaking to him; it sounded accusatory.

Three similar situations occurred between 1979 and 1983. He could not understand why people were suspecting him of murder. While working as a machinist at Photo-Etch in 1986, another employee told Ashbrook that he had many friends on the police force and knew one officer that could kick the shit out of him and put him in his place. Ashbrook felt intimidated and reported it to his employer, but it was not taken seriously. He quit his job and searched for another one.

For Ashbrook, life became a living hell. People continued to approach him about murders he had no information about. The stress took its toll in the workplace, resulting in quitting job after job. At one point, he believed the CIA was targeting him.

He contacted a local paper, the Fort Worth Weekly, to tell his story. He sent two letters, one on July 31, 1999, and the other August 10 of the same year, where he detailed how he had been approached by people who suspected him of murder and how the CIA was targeting him.

In August of 1999, Ashbrook went to a church looking for this man. He told the woman in the reception area that he was convinced the man was hiding there. The woman insisted that the person Ashbrook was looking for was not there. Before leaving the church, Ashbrook asked her if the church performed exorcisms.

Ashbrook's visit to the church and the conversation he'd had with the woman did happen. It is the only part of this story that is reality-based.

Ashbrook would visit one more church, and that visit would erupt into a bloody massacre.

Wedgwood Baptist

It was seven in the evening of September 15, and the Wedgwood Baptist Church was holding their annual event, "See you at the Pole." Organized by local schools, the event involved students affirming their faith by offering prayer as they gathered around the church's flag pole. They would pray for the resolution of the problems that confront society. The event featured a performance by Forty Days, a Christian Rock group. They were performing in the church's sanctuary, where approximately one hundred and fifty students had gathered to listen to their music.

As the celebration commenced, Ashbrook was lurking outside. He was dressed in everyday clothes; blue jeans and a black jacket.

He smoked incessantly. He was also packing; a loaded .9mm-Ruger semiautomatic pistol, a .380-caliber AMT pistol, six .9mm clips, and a pipe bomb.

He had bought the guns legally at a flea market.

Ashbrook walked into the church's lobby, where he encountered a woman. He showed her his guns. Terrified, the woman screamed, he shot her. He then turned his gun on a janitor, who had come to the woman's defense. He had already killed two.

The crowd of students was singing along to the songs with Forty Days. It was during their performance of the song, "Alle" that nineteen-year-old Drue Phillips heard several popping sounds. The bass player and backup singer for the band, Phillips thought the sounds were coming from the speakers. It was at that moment Ashbrook burst into the sanctuary. In a deliberate, calm, and steady manner, he started shooting.

Many people in the room thought Ashbrook was part of a skit, including Kevin Galey, the minister of counseling and community at the church. Galey was filming the event with a video camera. When he saw Ashbrook approaching two women, he positioned himself between them and Ashbrook, and continued to film Ashbrook.

Galey thought Ashbrook had a paint gun until Ashbrook shot him in the chest and pelvis. When Galey saw Ashbrook discard an empty clip and reload, he realized it was no skit. He also realized the blood running down his body was not paint.

Ashbrook started cursing and shouting anti-Baptist statements. He yelled for everyone to remain still. The crowd screamed as chaos broke out. People dove under the pews to take cover. Some of the students filmed Ashbrook as he went on a rampage. Those videos would later become useful when police conducted their investigation.

Ashbrook causally moved across the room, shooting those he selected as prey. He also threw a pipe bomb into the crowd. Amazingly, the pipe bomb did not explode correctly, so no one was harmed by it. Someone in the crowd yelled, 'run, run.' People ran for the exits.

Ashbrook unloaded thirty shells during the ten-minute mass shooting; it ended with him taking a seat in a pew and shooting himself in the head.

He had claimed the lives of seven people; four were teenagers. Another three people suffered major injuries.

IV

Sante Kimes

SANTE KIMES SAT IN THE PASSENGER SEAT AS HER son, Kenny Kimes, drove the Lincoln Town car. They had purchased the car from a dealer in Cedar City, Utah, using a bad check.

As usual, Sante was dressed in white, her hair styled just right, and plenty of make-up. The sixty-five-year-old mother had often been confused for Elizabeth Taylor in her younger years.

Kenny had recently dropped out of the University of Santa Barbara at his mother's urging, so he could be there for her more. Sante had groomed him since he was a child. She taught him how to steal, how to lie, and even how to kill. His mother was in full control of everything he did. The miles and years they left behind them were littered with forgery, theft, arson, fraud, and murder.

They were headed for Florida to carry out a scheme that would ultimately gain them nationwide attention, and a criminal trial where the presiding judge would refer to Sante as a "psychopath," and her son as a "remorseless predator."

Street Child

Born July 24, 1934, as Sante Louise Singhrs, Kimes was the child of Rattan and Mary Singhrs. Rattan was East Indian, while Mary was Irish. Sante had three siblings. The family moved to Southern California a few years later. Sante's father abandoned the family; it was an event that may have indirectly contributed to the life of crime that Sante would eventually lead.

Sante's mother supported her family by prostituting herself in Los Angeles. As a result, Sante spent her childhood in foster homes and orphanages but would constantly run away to search for her mother. It was on the streets of Los Angeles that she learned to steal to survive.

She was later adopted by a family and attended Carson high school, where she was active in extra-curricular activities, including cheerleading, working for the school newspaper, the Glee club, and the Spanish club. She was also very flirtatious and constantly sought the attention of boys in school. She came to the realization that her days of flirting in high school may have laid the foundation for her ability to masterfully control men. As for theft, that was a habit she continued to engage in, even when she was adopted by a loving family. She stole her adoptive father's credit card and went on a shopping spree. Her first arrest was in 1961 for petty theft.

Criminal Union

Sante's first experience in committing major crimes began when she married Kenneth Kimes, the father of her son. Kimes was her third husband.

Her first husband had been her high school sweetheart, Lee Powers. They got married three months after graduating in June 1952. The marriage lasted three months before divorcing him.

Her second marriage was to another classmate from high school, Edward Walker. Walker had always had a thing for Kimes, and they got married in 1956. They had a son. Walker divorced her in 1961 when she was arrested for petty theft. When she was released from jail, she supported herself through prostitution and stealing.

Kimes Sr. was a wealthy businessman who earned his fortune by developing motels and owning a construction company. A multimillionaire, Kimes Sr. was a shrewd strategist when it came to getting what he wanted, even if it meant breaking the law. He was also an alcoholic. He was so cunning that he was able to scam his way into attending a Washington fundraiser, where he and his wife got their picture taken with Vice President Gerald Ford and his wife.

Sante was living the high life. She and her husband had homes in California, Hawaii, Mexico, and the Bahamas. She worked as a Washington lobbyist, and in real estate development.

Sante got what she wanted from her marriage by grooming her husband just as she did with her son, though she employed a different strategy.

In the early stages of the marriage, she was like a geisha or a courtesan. She catered to his every need, sexually, and would shower him with flattery. She would also out-drink him. She would serve him whiskey while pouring herself a glass as well. Whenever he finished a drink, she would pour him and herself another one. What he did not notice was her pouring her drink into a potted plant when he wasn't looking. Eventually, he became so dependent on her that he would do anything she asked.

When it came to her son, she controlled his life from the time he was a child. Sante gave birth to Kenny on March 24, 1975; she was forty-one years old at the time. Kenneth was largely raised by nannies and never attended public school. Instead, he received private tutoring. Sante only allowed Kenneth to form friendships with children she approved of. If he had trouble finding friends, she would hire children, whom she found worthy, to be his friend.

When Kenny went off to college at UCSB, she followed him. She found a place for them to live off-campus and would co-host keg parties with her son. While traveling between the different homes the Kimes' owned, Sante would share her bed with her son, as her husband of advanced age slept alone.

Illegally Obsessed

Despite her rags to riches story, Sante could not resist the urge to commit crimes. In 1980, Sante stole a mink coat from another guest at the Mayflower's Town and County lounge. The other guest had it draped over a chair. Sante had her husband distract the woman by engaging in conversation while she stole it.

The couple also made false claims of items being stolen from their home and then provided inflated values for the items to the insurance company. Sometimes they committed arson on their own homes to collect. They were eventually arrested for the theft of the stolen mink coat. Sante and her husband posted four-thousand-dollar bail and escaped to Mexico, where they owned a home.

The Kimes' illegal activity took on an even darker nature when they got involved in false imprisonment and slavery. They would con Mexican girls into working as maids and servants in their homes, promising they would be well paid. For several years, they would illegally bring girls across the border to work for them, or they would entice those who were in the country already.

Those who fell for the trap found themselves being held captive in their homes. They were not allowed to wear shoes, and the doors were locked so they could not escape. They were frequently subjected to physical abuse and threats, and never received any payment for their work.

In their home in Mexico, one of the maids managed to escape and contacted authorities. Sante served five years in prison.

Prosecutors could not determine if her husband had been a willing participant or if he had been manipulated by Sante. As a result, he received a three-year suspended sentence and a seventy thousand dollar fine for his cooperation with the FBI.

Sante was released from prison in 1989; her husband passed away five years later. It was then she learned she had been left out of his will. Everything he owned went to his first wife and their children. Santa became determined to get as much of her deceased husband's wealth as possible. That decision would lead to a string of murders.

Sixty-three-year-old David Kazin had been a friend and business partner of Kenneth Kimes Sr. since the '70s. He had worked as an insurance claims adjuster but went on to open a photocopy business. In 1992, he received an unusual request from Kenneth Kimes Sr. Kimes asked him if he would be willing to take over the deed of his primary residence in California as he and Santa were facing a one hundred and fifty-thousand-dollar judgment from a lawsuit filed against them.

As time passed, Kazin requested Kimes Sr. take his name off the deed. Kimes Sr. agreed but never had it done, and then he died. Sante was aware of this and took out a two hundred and eighty-thousand-dollar mortgage on the home by forging Kazin's name on the loan documents. When Kazin discovered this, he threatened to report Sante to the police if she did not set things right. Kazin did not realize who he was messing with.

Sante told Kenny that Kazin was becoming a problem and that she needed him to take care of it. Those who entered Sante's orbit were doomed to grief, and Kazin would tragically find this out. He would join a list of Sante's victims. When Sante hired Doug Crawford to represent her in a civil suit filed by the families of her imprisoned "maids," his office was firebombed after Sante expressed her dissatisfaction with how he was handling the case. Another associate of Crawford, Elmer Holmgren, vanished mysteriously not long after the firebombing of Crawford's office.

Holmgren was an insurance adjustor, conned by Sante to burn down her Honolulu home so she could collect the insurance money. When the Bureau of Alcohol, Tobacco, and Firearms discovered what was happening, Holmgren became their informant as they worked their case for her arrest.

Killer Duo

On the evening of March 13, 1998, Kenny drove to Kazin's Los Angeles home, located in a quiet neighborhood nestled in Granada Hills. He brought an accomplice with him, and a .22 handgun.

Kenny was emotionless and did not speak as they made the thirty-minute drive. Kenny had learned long ago how not to feel. For him, his mother was the center of his world. When she wanted something, he jumped.

When they arrived at the home, they saw Kazin's Jaguar in the driveway. The property was surrounded by a wrought-iron gate. Kenny called Kazin to request he let him in, telling him he had come to resolve the issue with the deed. Kazin pushed the button that opened the gate. Kenny told his accomplice, Sean Little, to wait outside for him.

Sean waited less than two minutes before he heard gunshots. He ran up to the house. Kenny had a gun in his hand and was standing over Kazin's body. Kenny proceeded to clean the home to remove any clues that might incriminate them, or would indicate a struggle had occurred.

When they were done, they placed Kazin's body in the trunk of his Jaguar. Kenny drove the Jaguar toward Los Angeles Airport while Little followed in Kenny's car. As Kenny approached the airport, he saw an Avis rental car lot. He pulled into an alley adjacent to the car lot, and Little arrived seconds later. They tossed Kazin's body in a dumpster and drove away in Kenny's car, leaving the Jaguar near the Avis lot.

With Kazin out of the way, Sante made a phone call to Cedar City, Utah. Cedar City was the location of Parkway Motors. Jim Blackner was the sales manager there and had dealt with Kenneth Kimes for years, and he knew Sante. Sante told Blackner she wanted to purchase a Lincoln Town car. She wanted one with dark tinted windows. She agreed to a used, teal-green convertible and told Blackner she wanted it delivered to where she was staying, the Beverly Wilshire hotel. She agreed to trade her 1993 Lincoln and pay just under fifteen thousand dollars to make up the difference. Blackner delivered the car to Sante, feeling confident about the transaction since he knew who he was dealing with.

To Blackner's surprise, the check was returned for insufficient funds. When Blackner notified Sante, she was very apologetic and told him she would resubmit another check to him. Three weeks later, Blackner had still not received Sante's check; she then had the gall to call the car company to complain the trunk leaked. It was at that moment Blackner contacted Lynn Davis, a friend of his who worked for the Cedar City police.

Sante and Kenny got into the Lincoln Town car and took off from the Beverly Wilshire hotel; they were headed for Florida. They were on their way to pay a visit to Sayed Bilal Ahmed. Ahmed was an officer at the First Cayman bank. Her late husband had secret overseas accounts in the Bahamas and Grand Cayman.

Sante had been forging checks, using her husband's signature, to withdraw money from the accounts. Ahmed was getting suspicious and had agreed to meet with Sante for dinner at the hotel he was staying at in the Bahamas. When Sante and Kenny reached Florida, they took a boat to the Bahamas.

Upon their arrival, they took a taxi to a hotel in Cable Beach. When the two arrived, they surveyed the beach area. Sante was looking for a secluded area of the beach close to the hotel. Kenny saw just the spot, and Sante nodded approvingly. Kenny felt comforted that his mother had agreed with him and he had demonstrated his worth to her.

The two waited in their rooms until the evening. Sante dressed elegantly, as usual. Kenny wore a tailored suit. It was time. They went to Ahmed's room and knocked on the door. Ahmed was just finishing getting ready and invited the two into his room. Ahmed finished up his grooming.

Sante reached into her purse and withdrew a small bottle containing flunitrazepam, a powerful sedative. Sante gave it to Kenny, who poured the contents into a glass of bourbon Ahmed had left standing. When Ahmed came to join them, Sante told him he should finish his drink before they left. Ahmed finished off his drink.

The three went to the hotel's dining room and placed their orders. They could hear the pounding surf outside, punctuated by the beat of drums and the sound of guitars as a band played on the patio. Suddenly, Ahmed felt ill. He had difficulty speaking.

Sante and Kenny told Ahmed he should return to his room. The two helped him up and brought him back to his room. As Sante tried to comfort him, Kenny went into the bathroom and filled up the bathtub. When it was full, Kenny grabbed Ahmed and dragged him into the bathroom, lifted him up, and pushed him in the tub. He held Ahmed's head underwater as Ahmed struggled.

When Ahmed stopped moving, Kenny pulled him out of the bathtub and wrapped his body in a tarp. They waited until late evening when most of the hotel guests had retired to their room. When the time seemed right, Kenny went outside and found a homeless man. He offered him a large sum of money if he would be willing to help him load his car.

The man agreed and helped Kenny carry the rolled-up tarp to the car, which they placed in the backseat. True to form, Kenny and Sante took off without paying the man. They drove to the secluded spot they had identified earlier and dropped Ahmed's body into the sea.

The next morning, Sante and her son boarded the boat and took it back to Florida. It was on the boat that a woman started making conversation with Sante. The woman flattered Sante as to how much she resembled Elizabeth Taylor. Sante absorbed compliments like a sponge and felt it was worth her time to continue speaking with the woman. It turned out what the woman said next really got Sante's interest.

Silverman Murder

The woman told Sante she could tell she enjoyed living the high life and knew of a unique resort experience, located in New York City, which catered to the rich and powerful. As Sante listened, the wheels of her mind began turning out ideas for her next deadly plan.

Irene Silverman was an eccentric extrovert with a flamboyant flare, and very rich. She was once a famous ballerina, who had danced for the Rockettes, and the New York dance company. The eighty-three-year-old socialite's deceased husband was Samuel Silverman, a real estate mogul. During their marriage, her husband purchased the Beaux-Arts Mansion. He had left the six-story New York estate to Irene in his will. Always craving company, Silverman decided to share her home with others by turning it into Manhattan's premium-priced bed and breakfast, located on 20 East 65th Street. Celebrities who visited New York would pay rent of six thousand dollars per month to stay there.

Perched above the mansion's double front doors was a stone face carved into the gray limestone. The face wore a snarling expression with wings spread on each side of the head. Legend has it the face was carved at the beginning of the twentieth century, to stand guard against evil.

Unfortunately for Silverman, the mythological beast stood no chance against Sante. Sante worked her connections until she found someone who could perform a wiretap on Silverman's phones. This individual was also able to obtain Silverman's social security number and a sample of her signature. It was time to spring the trap!

It was the morning of July 5, 1998, and Silverman was dining with friends in the mansion's vast kitchen. Albanian fashion designer Elva Shkreli, and Carol Hanssen, Silverman's biographer, were eating dinner. As they ate, Silverman happened to look up at the closed-circuit security camera. Her friends noticed the expression of Silverman's face change. Silverman was normally cheerful, but an expression of concern surfaced. She had become suspicious of her new renter. The person on the security camera was Manny Guerin. As he entered the mansion, he was sure not to have his face revealed to the camera.

Kenny Kimes had shown up at the mansion, using the alias Manny Guerin. Kenny told Silverman that an old friend of hers had referred him to her. Silverman always had friends do reference checks on potential renters. As he was referred to her by her old friend, Silverman let her guard down. Besides, Kenny was sharply dressed, articulate, and seemed very proper. However, what impressed her more was that he pulled out six thousand dollars in cash. Her past renters always gave her a check. Taking cash payment would mean she could avoid reporting it to the Internal Revenue Service.

As tempting as it seemed, Silverman was hesitant. Those who knew Kenny often felt uncomfortable around him. He had a look in his eyes that seemed cold and unfeeling. Unfortunately for Silverman, greed overrode instinct, and she accepted the money. What irritated Silverman, even more, was when his "female assistant" showed up several days later.

Unlike soft-spoken Kenny, the elderly woman was loud with an abrasive-sounding voice. Silverman watched as the two moved out of range from the security camera. They appeared to be heading for his room. One of the conditions Silverman had given "Mr. Guerrin" was that he provide her with a form of identification, which he did not have when he first inquired about a room. Kenny had told Silverman he would provide it to her the following day. Three weeks had passed, and he still had not provided any form of identification.

Silverman told her guests they had better leave as she needed to speak to Mr. Guerrin. Silverman had given her sizable staff the weekend off because it was the July 4 holiday. Other than her "guests," she was the only one in the mansion. The Kimes were in a separate wing from the other guests.

The Kimes were planning to make their move late at night when they heard a knock on his door. Kenny opened the door to find Silverman. Silverman was frustrated with him as he had not yet provided her with identification. She informed him she was going to call the police to evict him and his assistant. Kenny could not believe his luck. Their prey had come to them. Kenny looked over his shoulder at his mother then smiled.

Kenny grabbed Silverman and pulled her into the room. Silverman panicked and screamed. At five feet, and eighty pounds, Kenny had no problem overpowering her. Sante grabbed the stun gun and zapped Silverman. She went through several convulsions before becoming still.

Kenny noticed she was still breathing, so he then strangled her with his bare hands. The old woman's eyes bulged out as she gurgled her last breath. Kenny released his grip and Silverman's head hit the floor with a thud, muffled by the thick carpet.

Smiling approvingly, Sante told her son to wrap Silverman's body in the shower curtain they had brought with them. Kenny placed the wrapped body in a large suitcase and awkwardly carried it out of the room as they made their way toward the mansion's front door.

As they exited the mansion, they experienced an unexpected silence. The lights in the neighboring houses were off as their residents had retired to bed. Central Park was just a block away. It was past midnight. The July 4 festivities were over. The only sound came from a few birds in the trees. They became startled when Kenny had slammed the trunk.

Sante barked at him for making so much noise. Timidly, Kenny apologized, though inside, he was resenting the way his mother had spoken to him. Nothing he ever did was good enough for her. He held in his anger as they pulled out of the driveway and took off toward New Jersey.

After dumping Silverman's body at a construction site, the Kimes drove back to New York. It was time to implement step two of Sante's plan. Sante had forged a deed that indicated Silverman had transferred ownership of the mansion to Atlantis Group Ltd., a shell corporation Sante had set up for this purpose. She would tell the workers at the mansion that Silverman had sold her the mansion and taken off for a lengthy vacation in Europe.

She had a more immediate task. She needed to contact Stann Patterson, an old friend who did odd jobs for them and helped them obtain guns. Before killing Silverman, Sante told him they would need his services.

Sante called him and told him to get to the mansion and act as the manager, while she and Kenny got out of town. She wanted to lay low for a while until things cooled off.

Capture

Unbeknownst to Sante, the FBI had contacted Patterson just before she placed that fateful call. They found out that Patterson had connections with Sante and wanted to question him about her involvement with the stolen Lincoln Town car and the death of Kazin, not to mention a few other crimes.

While Patterson was trusted by Sante, the FBI had offered him a sweet deal if he cooperated with them. They knew of his illegal gun sales and would not prosecute him. Patterson agreed and put on a bulletproof vest under his shirt and went off to meet Sante as they had previously planned.

The area around Sixth Avenue and 54th Street, where the New York Hilton was located, had undercover FBI agents strategically placed as they waited. Undercover officers from the New York Police were also there. Sante and Kenny arrived at the New York Hilton at seven in the evening; on the same day they had killed and dumped Silverman's body.

One of the FBI agents radioed the rest of the team that Sante had arrived in the stolen car. They waited until Patterson approached the car. As he leaned down to talk to Sante through her rolled-down driver's window, the FBI sprang into action and swarmed the car with guns raised.

Sante was enraged and protested her arrest, stating they had made a mistake. Kenny urinated in his pants.

Police handcuffed Sante and her son. Kenny was frightened not just for being caught; because he was being kept from his mother. The ruthless killer crumbled before the officers. When the police attempted to read him his Miranda rights, Kenny asked the officers to elaborate on each of the points. Kenny saw his mother being led away. Kenny yelled to her, 'Mom, what should I do?' His mother replied calmly, 'Everything will be okay.'

When law enforcement inspected the Lincoln Town car, they could not believe their good luck. The car was full of incriminating evidence that linked the Kimes to Silverman's disappearance. They found thirty thousand in cash, Silverman's passport, the keys to her mansion, a loaded Glock .9-mm pistol, a .22-Beretta, the empty box to a stun gun, her personal documents, handcuffs, fake deeds, and walkie-talkies.

As further details developed with time, officials began to suspect the Kimes' were involved in numerous other crimes. Sante was about to become one of the most infamous female criminals in U.S. history.

Convictions and Melodrama

Sante and Kenny both maintained their innocence as the prosecution and defense developed their cases. The prosecution had a big challenge to overcome: The bodies of Silverman and Ahmed had never been found.

The circumstantial evidence was overwhelming, and they did recover the body of Kazin. The prosecutor's case was getting stronger, so strong that Kenny changed his plea from innocent to guilty to avoid the death penalty. Kenny was willing to testify against his mother.

Sante remained firm in her plea of innocence and blamed Kenny, saying the only reason why he pled guilty was so that he could avoid the death penalty.

The trial began in the Spring of 2000. The elderly Sante was escorted into the courtroom by three armed guards. She turned the courtroom into a soap opera as she engaged in courtroom antics. She would continually accuse the justice system of conspiring against her and maintained that she was totally innocent. She would cry, throw tantrums, and even feigned a heart attack to interrupt the trial.

Whenever Kenny was led into the courtroom, Sante would give her shackled son a loving motherly smile while Kenny would dote over his mother. In one instance, Kenny reached for his mother's bun because a hair was out of place. Court security intervened, and from then on, mother and son were separated.

When it was time to return Kenny to his cell at Riker's Island, a guard placed him in handcuffs and he looked toward his mother, who was on the other side of the courtroom. 'Ma, 'I'll call you later,' he said.

Kenny's bizarre behavior reached the threshold in October 2000. Maria Zone, a reporter with television show Court T.V., entered Kenny's cell to interview him. Kenny had learned that he and his mother were being extradited to California to stand trial for the murder of Kazin.

Deeply upset, he grabbed Zone and held her hostage. He had taken her ballpoint pen and was holding its tip to her throat. Prison officials negotiated for four hours for her release. At one point, an official was able to distract Kenny while another grabbed Zone, and brought her to safety.

During the Kazin trial in June 2004, Kenny initially pleaded innocent but later pled guilty, a plea agreement that would avoid him or his mother getting the death penalty. His mother continued to deny any involvement.

When both trials ended, Kenny was convicted of the first-degree murder of Silverman, while Sante was convicted of first-degree murder of Kazin. There was not enough evidence to get a conviction for the death of Ahmed. Besides the murders, the juries found Sante guilty of fifty-eight other charges, and Kenny was found guilty of sixty additional charges, including conspiracy, grand larceny, burglary, forgery, eavesdropping, and illegal weapon possession.

Sante was sentenced to Bedford Hills Correctional Facility for Women, located in New York, for one hundred and twenty years.

Twenty-five-year old Kenny received one hundred and twenty-five years and four months.

Sante died in prison at age seventy-nine.

Authorities suspected the Kimes had been involved in other murders and crimes but lacked proof.

V
Robert James Acremant

DARLENE BRADSHAW SAT IN HER LIVING ROOM watching the local evening news.

Bradshaw had moved to Medford, Oregon, from Stockton, California after she separated from her husband. Her son, Robert, was five years old at the time.

She was trying to rebuild her relationship with her son, who was older now and living there.

The news opened with an update on the murder of two women. They had been shot, and their bodies were found in an abandoned pick-up truck.

In a fraction of a second, Bradshaw's emotions went from intrigued to shocked. The newscast displayed the sketch artist's portrait of the killer.

It was her son. She just knew it. Bradshaw contacted her ex-husband.

How could it be her son? Robert had honorably served in the air force. It was her son, whose friends and supervisors all described as hard-working, focused, competent, courteous, and with a desire to be successful.

While most of the guys in the military were partying, Acremant would go to school at the Holloman Air Force base. His exceptional work ethic allowed him to complete an MBA from Golden Gate University within two years, which he had attended after leaving the military. He had the goal of retiring at thirty-five.

Meanwhile, three hundred and fifty-five miles away in Stockton, California, Robert Acremant was hiding out in his room at Motel 6. The darkness within him that had remained dormant had eclipsed any memory of who he once was. He had reached the other side of that darkness. However, he did not stay in the room like a scared animal. Rather, he stopped caring about what was about to happen to him as the SWAT team surrounded his room and stormed inside.

This all came about because of his infatuation with a stripper.

An Unlikely Killer

Acremant was born on May 9, 1968, in Stockton, California. His father, Ken Acremant was a bartender. His mother was an accountant. They lived in a ranch house that had been in the family for one hundred and forty years.

He realized early on that there were bigger things for him than Stockton could offer. A blue-collar town, Stockton always lagged behind economically from the rest of California. Its inequality gap only grew larger as more young people moved to the bigger cities, such as San Francisco.

In 1991, after leaving the military and graduating from Golden Gate University, Acremant worked for Roadway Express in their Southern California office as an efficiency expert.

For all of his achievements and go-getter attitude, Acremant felt like an empty vessel. He had tried all his life to achieve and gain the recognition he desired from his parents.

His parents' divorce when he was a young child had left him with a deep insecurity that he was not good enough. While the military and school provided structure and something to focus on, he was now on his own. Another object of uncertainty loomed over him as he was worried about his job. Because of the economic downturn, he feared he would be laid off. Between his time in the military and school, Acremant had few friends. He spent most of his time alone studying, going to the library, or going for hikes. His experience with women was very limited.

Acremant decided he needed a break; the walls of his modest California apartment were closing in on him. He drove to Las Vegas. While driving, an idea came to him. He decided he was going to quit his job and start a software company. What would it be like to have a successful company? He thought of how it would feel showing his parents he had achieved his goal of retiring by age thirty-five. If that did not impress them, what would?

Ecstasy

As Acremant entered Las Vegas's northern city limits, he noticed a strip club on the side of the road, the Palomino Club. He parked, entered the club, found a table, and ordered a drink from an attractive and scantily-clad waitress.

Having this woman be so friendly to him was enjoyable, and the dark atmosphere of the club made him feel safe. The fear of rejection that always haunted him faded away as he spoke to the waitress. As the waitress walked away, there was a dancer finishing her number and heading backstage. Acremant did not have much of a chance to watch her because he was focusing on the waitress. The D.J. announced the next dancer; Ecstasy.

Her entrance caught his attention immediately. She seemed so confident, in control, and oozing sensuality. As she started her performance, she made eye contact with Acremant and gave him a sexy smile. He was transfixed by her very suggestive moves. When her number was completed, she retreated backstage only to reappear on the club floor a few minutes later.

She sauntered over to him and spoke to him briefly, small talk before asking him if he would like a table dance. Eagerly, he grabbed his wallet and paid her ten dollars. As she danced erotically before him, he was transported to another world. All of his problems and worries erased from his mind. When she finished her dance, she socialized with him and asked if he would like another dance. He took her up on her offer. Between his drinks and her dances, he had spent five hundred dollars. He was hooked. It was the beginning of his downfall.

Every chance he got, he returned to Vegas to see Ecstasy. Each time he continued to spend excessive amounts of money. While he was working at Roadway Express, he was earning a salary of fifty thousand per year. A few months later, he returned to Las Vegas as the owner of his own software company. As his company started to take off, he was spending upwards of fifteen hundred dollars per visit to the club. For him, Ecstasy became a drug that elevated him to a different orbit, where he found total escape.

While she found him attractive, it was all about business for Ecstasy. She had found a source of revenue in him, and she played him for what it was worth. Eventually, she agreed to go out with him for lunch. Acremant learned that her real name was Alla Kosova, and she was from Russia.

Acremant started to believe that they were developing a relationship, while Kosova always kept it professional and never allowed their interaction to turn romantic. For her, the occasional lunch or dinner was just a way to keep him interested.

Desperation

In 1995, Acremant experienced his world crumbling. While his software company had taken off at the beginning, the technology bubble had caught up with him. Investors were excessive in their speculation as to the value of technological companies, and the market was correcting. The reality for the tech world hit hard, and as with many start-up companies, Acremant's company went bankrupt.

He then had trouble finding a job. Because he could no longer splurge at the Palomino, Kosova's interest in him faded rapidly. Acremant, who did not handle alcohol well, began to drink excessively. His sense of escape that he got from Kosova's attention had crashed and burned. His demons could no longer be tamed by her, and he became depressed.

Acremant couldn't afford to live in Los Angeles and decided to move to Visalia, California, in October of 1995. A small community within the San Joaquin Valley, Visalia, is located one hundred and ninety miles north of Los Angeles.

Acremant found a small studio apartment there. The night he moved in, Acremant went out to find a bar. As he drove around, he was surprised to see someone he knew, Scott George. Twenty-three-year-old George was the son of one of his mother's friends. The two of them went drinking. The loss of Kosova and his company, mixed with his anger and the alcohol, had rendered him numb to life.

During their drive home, Acremant pulled off the road into a secluded area. George wondered what he was doing when Acremant pulled out a gun. George looked terrified as Acremant angrily expressed all the shit he was going through. While pleading for Acremant to put away the gun, Acremant gave him an evil look, a look devoid of any feeling, and pulled the trigger.

George fell backward, his body hitting the passenger door before falling sideways. Acremant saw that he was still alive. George began to vomit. Infuriated that he vomited in his car, Acremant shot him a second time in the head and cursed him for messing up his car.

Acremant drove for two hours before he reached his father's ranch. He tossed George's body in an abandoned mine shaft on his father's property. Acremant would later be questioned by investigators as to how he felt shooting someone. His response was, 'Nothing. It is like shooting a wall.'

As he drove away, he could think of only one thing: He needed to win Kosova back. To do that, he would need money. Acremant once saw a movie starring Al Pacino. In the movie, Pacino's character made the statement, *'When you get money, you get power.*

And when you get power, you get women.' For Acremant, this quote became his mantra.

Murder in Medford

On December 4, 1995, Roxanne Ellis was in her office, getting ready for a showing at eleven in the morning. The fifty-three-year-old Ellis was co-owner of a property management company. Her partner, both at work and in private, was forty-two-year-old Michelle Abdill. Ellis was a mother and politically active in fighting for gay rights and volunteered her time helping AID patients.

Ellis left her office and drove to the apartment at Sheraton Court to meet her client, located in Medford, Oregon. The apartment was in a community, much like Visalia, an agricultural community with numerous wineries that doted on its green countryside. The client she was meeting was Acremant. Ellis had shown the apartment to Acremant the previous week, but he wanted another show. She found Acremant to be an attractive man and enjoyed their conversation during the last showing. When she arrived at the apartment, she saw Acremant waiting for her. Parking her pick-up truck, she got out, and the two entered the apartment.

Ellis's daughter, Lori Ellis, was getting worried. She had made several attempts to contact her mother but did not receive a call or text back, which was uncharacteristic of her. In the past, she always responded back within seconds. Lori called the management company and expressed her concern to Abdill. Abdill was also concerned as Ellis had missed her two o'clock showing. Sometime later, Lori got a call back from Abdill, who told her she had received a call from Ellis and that her car battery had died. She told Lori she would be driving out to assist her.

As they entered the apartment, Acremant closed the door behind him and pulled out a .25-caliber pistol with a homemade silencer attached. She stared at him in shock. He ordered her to get out her checkbook and write him checks for a total of fifty thousand dollars from their business account. Crying from fear and with a shaking hand, she wrote the first check and handed it to him.

Acremant grabbed the check as a nervous smile appeared on his face, but it did not last. She watched the expression on his face turn to anger when he looked at the check. Printed in the corner were the words "for deposit only." It was at that moment Abdill walked into the apartment.

She was stunned to see Acremant pointing his gun at Ellis. He ordered both of them to get into Ellis's truck. Ellis never had battery trouble. Acremant had made her call Abdill to tell her that so she would not be suspicious about missing her other appointment.

Lori grew concerned when she had still not received word from her mother or Abdill, and decided to drive to the apartment herself. As she approached the apartment, she saw her mother's truck pull away. She followed her truck and could not understand why her mother was not slowing down or stopping. She beeped her horn and flashed her lights. Instead of stopping, the truck raced off. Lori knew that something was very wrong.

Upon receiving Lori's call, police started searching the area around the apartment and questioned the neighbors. Some had witnessed a white male casing the apartment a few days earlier. He had even approached one of them, introducing himself as their new neighbor. Police began to wonder if the disappearance of the two women had anything to do with their sexual orientation.

Acremant ordered the driver to pull over in a secluded area of the highway. He jumped out of the passenger side and ordered the two to get out. He made them get in the truck bed and lie down. While keeping his gun pointed at her, he ordered Ellis to do the same. The trembling women lay side by side, in the truck bed, sobbing. He tied each of them up and covered their mouths with duct tape. The women's muffled sobs filled the otherwise silent air. Both women intuitively knew what was going to happen next. Acremant shot both of them in the back of the head, execution-style. Because he had a silencer on the gun, no one heard the shots.

The next day, a cable T.V. repairman made the gruesome discovery and called Medford police.

Acremant had come up empty in his robbery attempt. He was growing even more desperate; he needed money so that he could regain Kosova's attention. On December 12, he drove back to Visalia, to the home of Taryn Sweeny, a friend of the family. Twenty-two-year-old Sweeney was getting ready to go out with a girlfriend when she heard a knock on the door. Opening the door, she was surprised to see Acremant.

Before any words could be exchanged, Acremant forced himself inside and grabbed her. He placed his hand over her screaming mouth and told her that he wanted her mother's jewelry and that he would not hurt her if she cooperated. Agreeing to cooperate, he released his grip on her so she could go to her mother's room. It was at that moment the doorbell rang. Sweeney screamed, 'he is going to kill me!' She rushed for the door. Unsure what to do, Acremant's hesitation provided her with the amount of time she needed to run away with her friend.

One Last Time

He had made two robbery attempts and failed to collect any money. Plus, he had left three people dead; however, that fact was not of any concern to him. Even the idea he might get caught was of secondary importance to him. On top of his list was Kosova. The next day, he decided to sell his car. He got five thousand dollars. He rented a U-Haul truck and drove to Las Vegas.

Acremant felt a sense of relief as he entered the strip club. Kosova was surprised to see him and went over to talk to him. By the time he left the club, he had spent over four thousand dollars. He took her to lunch, and as they ate, Kosova could not help but feel something was not right. She asked him why he was driving a U-Haul truck. Acremant told her that he would explain it all when they left the restaurant. After paying the check, they returned to the U-Haul truck and got in. Acremant told her he had killed three people in the last week and showed her the gun he had used.

Kosova was terrified that she was next but managed to stay calm. She told him she loved him and he needed to get away to avoid capture. Telling him that she loved him probably saved her life. If he had felt rejected, she probably would have ended up as his next victim.

When Acremant had been hired at the Roadway Express, his father had given him a family heirloom, a diamond ring his father's father had owned since he was sixteen. Acremant returned to Stockton to visit his father. He told his father he loved him and handed him the ring before leaving. His father did not know what to make of it until the telephone rang; it was his son's mother.

Darlene told him about the news story and that she was certain their son was the killer. She told him she had contacted the Medford police. Ken got in his car, took off looking for his son. As he was driving, he spotted the U-Haul truck parked at a Motel 6 nearby. He contacted Stockton police, who had been notified by the Medford police he might be in the area.

On December 13, a SWAT team from Stockton police descended on the motel and apprehended Acremant without any resistance.

Acremant appeared in the Jackson County court on September 11, 1996, and pled guilty to murdering Roxanne Ellis and Michelle Abdill.

He was sentenced to death in 1997, but his death sentence was overturned in 2011 because there were questions regarding his mental competency. Experts for the defense diagnosed him as paranoid schizophrenic in 2002, while experts for the prosecution could not rule it out.

An agreement was made that if it was discovered later that Acremant had feigned mental illness, the death penalty could be reinstated. Acremant was also sentenced to death in California for the murder of Scott George on October 3, 2002. He is currently living out a life sentence in the Oregon State Penitentiary.

During the trial, his father and Kosova testified against him.

VI
Josephine Victoria Gray

IT WAS 1991, AND MONTGOMERY COUNTY prosecutors were hanging their heads.

Murder trials of Josephine Gray and Clarence Goode were scheduled to start in just a few days, and the witnesses scheduled to testify had suddenly recanted their confessions or had disappeared.

Without witness testimony, the case against Gray and Goode was weak. They lost the cooperation of their witnesses when Gray and Goode were granted bail. Why were Gray and Goode offered bail? It was because prosecutors could not link the murders to them and because of who Gray was.

At the time, she was a forty-five-year-old grandmother who had grandchildren and had worked as a school janitor for the last seventeen years. She had also opened up a children's daycare center in her home. Convincing a jury that she killed her last two husbands would be difficult.

Now that their witnesses were refusing to testify, their case against her would have to be dismissed. Why were their witnesses no longer cooperating? It was because Gray, also known as the "black widow," practiced voodoo. They were afraid she would place a curse on them. But the prosecutors were not willing to give up pursuing Gray, and Gray was not giving up killing!

A Killer Lifestyle

Josephine Gray was born in 1946 and lived in Maryland. The home she had lived in for the last eleven years was located in a working neighborhood of Upper Marlboro. She was the mother of six children and eleven grandchildren. An African American, Josephine worked as a janitor at Richard Montgomery High School, located in the 17700 Block of Stoneridge Drive. From the time she was twenty, she'd cleaned restrooms and gym floors. She continued working to the age of fifty-seven; when she retired.

She was a flamboyant woman who wore heavy makeup, tight skirts, and drove fancy cars, including a Cadillac Eldorado and a Chrysler New Yorker. She also went on shopping sprees at high-end stores like Saks Fifth Avenue. How does a retired janitor live a celebrity lifestyle? For Josephine, the answer was simple: She killed for her lifestyle.

Josephine knew how to control and dominate those around her, especially the men in her life. With her scheming mind and sensuous ways, Josephine attracted men into her web of deceit. Once they entered her lair, she gradually took control of them and had them do her bidding.

The First Husband

Josephine's lethal activities began in 1974, with her first husband, Norman Stribbling. Josephine was unhappy with their marriage, as he was abusive toward her. Josephine felt trapped in the marriage and had an affair with another man, William Robert Gray. Gray was in his thirties, married, and had six children. She had met him through work, as they both worked for the same company that provided janitorial cleaners to businesses.

She was so sick of being married to Stribbling that she knew she had to get him out of her life. However, she could not just divorce him. She was listed as the beneficiary on his insurance policy, through John Hancock Mutual Life Insurance.

One morning as Stribbling and Josephine were lying in bed, Josephine decided it was time to get rid of him. She pulled out a handgun from her night table and attempted to shoot him, but her gun misfired. Stribbling ran out of the house in a sheer panic. He told some of his family that Josephine had tried to shoot him but did not follow-up with the police.

Josephine talked to several acquaintances and tried to solicit them to kill her husband, but they would not accept her offer. She decided that she would try to recruit her lover, William.

Josephine traveled to Flatbush, New York, to the Voodoo supply store she frequented. She picked up some powders and herbs and brought them back to her home, where she prepared a mixture. That night, she went to William's home and added her mixture to his food. He ate the food without detecting the mixture.

William did not know it, but his spiked food would result in his mind becoming more susceptible to her suggestions; adding some sensuous touching to her persuasion did not hurt either. William agreed to kill Stribbling for her.

It was two weeks after his wife had attempted to shoot him that Stribbling returned to their home. Josephine had called him and apologized for what she had done, explaining that she was delusional at the time. Stribbling was tired of staying at friends' homes and agreed to return.

Upon returning to the home, he knocked on the door, and Josephine, who was dressed in a revealing gown, invited him in. She grabbed his hand and led him to the bedroom; William was waiting and pointing a gun at him. Stribbling knew what was going to happen this time; he was going to die.

William ordered Stribbling to get in his car and told him to drive to River Road, which was close to Stribbling's home. As he drove, Stribbling was overcome with fear. He begged William to let him go, and that he would give him everything he had, including his car. William told him to shut up and drive as he kept the gun pointed at him. By chance, Stribbling looked up at the rearview mirror and noticed the headlights of a car following them. Because it was dark, he could not make out the car or its driver.

When they reached a secluded area along River Road, William ordered Stribbling to pull over and park the car. William placed the gun to the right side of Stribbling's head. It was at that point there was the sound of a car door closing. A few seconds later, Stribbling saw Josephine peering at him through the passenger window. She seemed to have a hint of a smile on her face. "What are you waiting for?" she asked William. William pulled the trigger. The bullet traveled through Stribbling's head and exited the left side, sending blood splattering all over the driver side window.

They took his wallet, so it would appear that his murder was the result of a robbery, and then took off in her car. As they drove, Josephine looked at William with a smile. Stribbling's body was discovered on March 3, 1974. A few days later, Josephine made a claim with John Hancock Insurance and received a check for sixteen thousand dollars.

During the investigation, authorities interviewed members of the family and acquaintances and discovered that some of them were approached by Josephine to commit the murder. Both Josephine and William were charged with the murder of Stribbling; however, the charges were eventually dropped as witnesses stopped cooperating with authorities when Josephine was released on bail.

They had received threats from Josephine, warning them against testifying.

Friends and family knew of Josephine's involvement with Voodoo. The matriarch of the family, Josephine, had dominated and controlled her family by playing on the fears they had of her dark magic. The friends, who took Stribbling in when he'd fled from his wife's attack, shared with authorities their own terrifying experience.

They told of how they found Stribbling in their bathroom with his face covered in blood. He had gouged his face with his fingernails. He could not explain why he had mutilated his face, just that his mind was ordering him to do so. They later found a voodoo doll in his room. How it got there was anyone's guess.

The Second Husband

In August of 1975, Josephine and William used the insurance money as a down payment for a house they bought in Gaithersburg. Three months later, they were married. William took out an insurance policy through Minnesota Mutual; it would cover the cost of the mortgage payments should he pass away. It provided security for Josephine. He also took out an accidental death insurance policy through another insurance company, Life Insurance Company of North America. Josephine was the beneficiary of that, as well.

The stage was set for the next scene in Josephine's twisted play; the black widow was ready to strike again.

Josephine began an affair while married to William. Her affair was with her younger cousin, twenty-three-year-old Clarence Goode. Goode had come to live with Josephine because he was having trouble getting his life together. He had been working for Loomis Armored Inc., an armored car service. Traveling through Baltimore, he went from relative to relative, trying to find someone willing to put him up for a while.

Josephine used this opportunity to gain control over him. She made him dependent on her by providing him with sex, while at the same time, controlling his every move. She took away his phone, would not let him work, nor could he leave the house without her.

It was at the time of this affair she also turned the tables on William, by exerting her intimidation over him. She showed up at his workplace, swung a baseball bat at him, as well as threatened him with a screwdriver.

In the summer of 1990, William moved out of their home and got his own apartment in nearby Germantown. He also filed a complaint with authorities, stating that he believed his wife was trying to kill him. He also claimed that Goode had threatened him with a .9mm handgun.

Besides reporting it to the police, he began the process of removing Josephine as the beneficiary of his life insurance.

On October 5, 1990, William appeared in court to testify against Josephine and Goode, but the case was re-scheduled. That evening, William was driving home when he noticed Josephine's car following him. She was flashing her lights at him.

Though he was apprehensive, he pulled over to the side of the road. Josephine pulled up alongside him. It was then Goode sat up from the passenger seat, pointing a .45-caliber handgun at him. William shifted his car in reverse and managed to drive away. William instinctively knew that he was in deep trouble.

Josephine had found out William was in the process of removing her as a beneficiary on his life insurance and realized she needed to act fast before the change in policy took effect.

On November 9, one week before the trial date was scheduled, William returned home from work at Clopper Mills Elementary School, where he worked as a building service manager. It was two-thirty in the afternoon when he entered his apartment and came face-to-face with Goode, who had a gun pointed at him.

Without a word, Goode pulled the trigger, hitting him in the neck. The second shot hit William in the chest. Goode waited and watched William die, his blood freely flowing out of his body and onto the living floor. Without any remorse, Goode left the apartment.

In the spring of 1991, Josephine and Goode were both arrested and charged with William's murder. When questioned by detectives, Josephine showed no emotion. Because they lacked any physical evidence connecting her to the murder, she and Goode were released on bond.

That was also the moment when witnesses again stopped cooperating with authorities. While looking for clues in William's apartment, they found a Voodoo doll with pins in it. The charges were dropped, and Josephine later collected fifty-four thousand dollars from William's insurance policies, as the value of the policy had exceeded the amount owed on the mortgage. She had managed to collect even though she was being considered as a suspect in William's murder.

During the early 1990s, Josephine and Goode lived together; however, it would only be a matter of time before Josephine's insatiable greed would rise to the surface once more. Unbeknownst to Josephine, her reign of terror was approaching the end, and it would be her insatiable greed that would do her in.

The Boyfriend

As with her previous two husbands, Josephine was becoming tired of her live-in boyfriend, Goode. At some point in their relationship, Goode was no longer the passive boyfriend, who had allowed himself to be ordered around by Josephine. Goode blackmailed Josephine, threatening to report her to authorities if she did not share some of the wealth from the insurance fraud.

On March 5, 1996, Goode applied for a life insurance policy from Interstate Assurance Company. The one hundred-thousand-dollar policy had Josephine as the sole beneficiary, should he pass away.

Josephine now had plenty of reasons to get Goode out of her life. She started to plot her next scheme to get rid of him; by doing what had always worked for her, finding another man to do the dirty work.

Andre Savoy was Josephine's new lover, whom she was having an affair with while still with Goode. Josephine always chose a certain kind of man. She picked men who were quiet, compliant, enjoyed drinking, and watching television. It did not take much from her to get them to take the bait and reel them in. All she had to do was to use her sexuality.

In June 1996, a letter from Interstate Assurance addressed to Goode arrived in the mail at Josephine's address, intercepted by her. The letter indicated that Goode had a sixty-day grace period before the policy would be canceled due to non-payment.

Josephine knew it was time to get rid of Goode.

On June 21, 1996, Josephine told Goode to drive her to some stores, as she wanted to buy some clothing. They left in his car early and returned home late afternoon. They pulled into the garage and were about to get out of the car when Josephine told Goode to close the garage door first. Goode looked puzzled by this request but did as he was told. The garage door closed shut, and the two exited the car. Savoy emerged from behind some storage boxes. He had a gun in his hand, pointed at Goode.

Goode looked terrified and turned to Josephine, who gave him an evil smile and stepped into the house. As she did, she told Savoy, "You know what to do."

Without a word or any sense of hesitancy, Savoy pulled the trigger and shot Goode in the head. Goode's body collapsed to the garage's cold and barren concrete floor. He was killed instantly. He died with his eyes wide open and a fearful expression on his face, as a pool of blood formed beneath him.

Savoy saw the door to the house open; it was Josephine who had come to check on him. She nodded approvingly and told Savoy to put Goode's body in the trunk of his car and get rid of it. She also pointed to a commercial vacuum cleaner in the corner of the garage. She told him to use it to clean up the floor.

When Goode's body was loaded in the trunk, Savoy drove it to West Baltimore, where he abandoned the car at 2303 Avalon Street. Josephine picked him up and brought him back to the house. Goode's body was discovered the same day by Baltimore police, with a .9mm bullet in his head.

Changing Tactics

The Montgomery County police served a search warrant for Josephine's home but, in the end, could not come up with the physical evidence to link her to Goode's murder. As a result, she was never charged. Josephine may have felt she had outsmarted police and that she had, once again, committed the perfect murder. However, she was wrong. What she did not realize was that federal authorities were after her, and they had wire-tapped her phones.

The Montgomery County police understood their dilemma. They knew Josephine was guilty of three murders but lacked hard evidence to prove it. With witnesses too fearful to cooperate, the police turned to federal agents, who were pursuing her on federal fraud charges. Their burden of proof was not as great as state murder charges. By charging her with fraud, federal authorities did not have to prove she had killed the men; rather, they only had to prove she'd had a role in their deaths. Additionally, these federal charges would enable them to hold her without bail.

Josephine filed a claim with Interstate Assurance as the beneficiary of the policy, but Interstate Assurance would not make payment as she was a suspect in Goode's murder. Two years later, she still was not charged for Goode's murder, and the decision of who was the proper beneficiary of the policy went through litigation. There was a settlement, and Josephine received ninety-nine thousand dollars in benefits. The remaining benefits went to Goode's son. The two-year legal battle had all begun with a phone call Josephine had made to Interstate Assurance.

Federal agents had been listening to every word.

Federal agents built their case, and on December 5, 2001, a federal judge ordered Josephine held without bond.

On January 5, 2002, Josephine was charged with collecting insurance proceeds after causing the death of two husbands along with Goode. The following day, Montgomery County police charged her with two counts of first-degree murder for the killing of her two husbands.

Josephine was fifty-five at the time. Because she was being held without bail for federal crimes, witnesses were coming forward, including Savoy, who testified that Josephine had tried to kill him the previous summer and had applied for life insurance on him.

Even while being held in a federal detention center, Josephine had the gall to call Savoy and tell him to claim the Fifth Amendment when being questioned.

After having escaped justice for twenty-eight years, the woman who had become known as the "black widow" had finally been snagged by the web of justice.

Her trial began on July 29, 2002. On August 17, 2002, Josephine was found guilty of eight counts of mail and wire fraud by a jury of the U.S. District Court in Greenbelt.

During her insurance schemes, she had collected a total of one hundred and sixty-five thousand dollars.

She received the maximum sentence of forty years in prison and was ordered to repay one hundred and seventy thousand dollars.

Conclusion

IN GREEK MYTHOLOGY, ICARUS WAS GIVEN WINGS made by his father. They were constructed of wax and feathers. His father gave him the wings so he could escape the island of Crete but warned him that he needed to keep his distance from the sun. Icarus ignored his father's warning.

Out of his hubris and complacency, he flew to the sun, only to fall helplessly to the sea when his wings melted. There is a bit of Icarus in all the killers in this book.

Michael David Clagett was a wellspring of complacency as he allowed his even more sinister girlfriend to use him to do her bidding.

Aaron Alexis was poisoned by his own hubris in thinking his personal sufferings justified him committing a vicious attack on the Washington Navel Center.

The same kind of hubris led Larry Gene Ashbrook to take the lives of students and staff at the Wedgwood Baptist Church.

Sante and Kenny Kimes exhibited extreme hubris in that they had money, but felt they deserved more.

Robert James's hubris was dramatically described in his motive for killing; feed his addiction for a lap dance.

For Josephine Victoria Gray, her hubris of money was stronger than the value of human life.

We are biologically wired to avoid painful situations and pursue situations we perceive will lead to our happiness. Somewhere in their murderous minds, these killers believed their hope for happiness required eliminating the lives of those who they perceived as getting in their way.

While their actions may seem inconceivable to us, they made sense to them. For them, killing was a means to an end. People who commit mass killings frequently believe they have been wronged and are aching to take revenge. They feel their actions are justified, even if their targets have no relation to their original victimization.

The killers profiled in this book felt isolated from the rest of the world. Because of this, anyone was a potential target of their hatred. These killers flew too close to the sun. Unlike Icarus, however, they took others with them on their downward spiral.

As long as our society underfunds mental health programs, stigmatizes the mentally ill, and allows easy access to guns, we will continue to experience the explosions that come from the brewing anger of those with murderous minds.

Acknowledgments

This is a special thanks to the following readers who have taken time out of their busy schedule to be part of True Crime Seven Team. Thank you all so much for all the feedbacks and support!

Judith Sentyz, Wanda Shattuck, Merle Ohpa, Tara Pendley, Kathy Morgan, Pamela Culp, Barbara Davis, Anna McCown, Naomi Burney, Linda Wheeler, Joan Baker, Linda F. Jones, Donna R., Tonja Marshall, Dannii D, Susan Leedy, James Herington, Elizabeth A Norris, Catherine Hodges Scarboro, Timothy W. Haight, Tina Gaddy

Continue Your Exploration Into

The Murderous Minds

Excerpt From Murderous Minds Volume 2

I

Edward Charles Allaway

HE FELT IT WAS THE ONLY WAY; IT WAS THE next necessary step.

On July 12, 1976, shortly before nine in the morning, Edward Charles Allaway entered the Hilton Hotel in Anaheim, California. He picked up a phone and called 911. "I went berserk at Cal State Fullerton, and I committed some terrible acts. I'd appreciate it if you people would come down and pick me up. I'm unarmed, and I'm giving myself up to you."

He hung up the phone, entered the hotel's banquet room, and waited for the police to arrive.

Within minutes, he could hear the sound of sirens approaching. He could also hear his heart beating as he waited; yet, a strange feeling of relief descended upon him.

The SWAT team stormed the banquet room and took him down. Meanwhile, the bodies of seven of his co-workers lay dead in the library at Cal State.

Thirty-seven-year-old Allaway, a custodian at the California State University at Fullerton, had just committed the worst mass murder in the history of Orange County, as of that date.

Paranoia Unleashed

Allaway was born in 1939 in Royal Oak, Michigan, a suburb of Detroit. His family was poor and lived in a small apartment above a grocery store. He had an alcoholic father, and one sibling, a sister.

When he grew older, Allaway joined the Marines, but his service was brief as he was dishonorably discharged. Due to his oppositional nature, he spent many years bouncing from job to job. He was continuously getting fired for fighting with his co-workers.

Growing up, his parents noticed him engaging in odd behaviors but never addressed it. The person who did confront him about these behaviors was his first wife, Carol. Allaway acted in a paranoid manner and repeatedly accused her of sleeping with other men and posing for pornographic movies. He assaulted her and threatened her with a knife, telling her that he would cut her up if she ever left him. Carol convinced him to seek help, which he did. He spent a month in a mental institution in Dearborn, where he underwent electric shock therapy.

In 1973, Carol left him. A few days later, he moved to Orange County in Southern California. His sister lived there and worked as a secretary in the sociology department at California State Fullerton. Only a few months after arriving in Orange County, Allaway married Bonnie, his second wife. Allaway and his new wife spent the next two years traveling around the country, supporting themselves by doing odd jobs as they traveled.

However, their dream of traveling around the country did not work out as they could not support themselves, which frustrated Allaway. A loner at heart, he did not want to deal with co-workers. They returned to Orange County, and Bonnie got a job working at the Hilton Hotel in Anaheim, while Allaway's sister got him a job as a custodian at the university's library in 1975.

Though he had left Michigan, Allaway's demons did not remain there; they followed him to Orange County and reappeared with a vengeance.

Allaway's Meltdown

Allaway was extremely jealous, and as with his first wife, he accused Bonnie of cheating on him. He also threatened her with a knife, telling her that he would cut up her face if she ever cheated on him.

At work, his co-workers found him to be irritable whenever they interacted with him. This was especially true with minorities. Allaway was a racist and resented blacks and Hispanics. It bothered him when his co-workers offered suggestions on how to approach a task, especially if they were not Caucasian. He was upset when the university hired a Mexican-American from outside the University for the position of lead custodian, particularly when a white co-worker had applied for the same position.

In the basement of the library was a room called the Instructional Media Center. Some of the janitors would bring pornographic movies from home and view them there during off-hours.

Allaway did not realize he had paranoid schizophrenia; this diagnosis would only be determined after the massacre. His hallucinations led him to believe not only were his co-workers forcing Bonnie to perform in pornographic films, but they were also after him.

His paranoia at work was exasperated when Bonnie left him on Memorial Day in 1976. She could not take Allaway's abuse any longer. Allaway became sullen, his anger hitting a threshold.

He went to K-Mart, in Buena Park, and purchased a .22-caliber semi-automatic rifle and ammunition. In his mind, there was only one thing that he could do about the situation.

The Attack

Just after seven in the morning on July 12, 1976, Allaway drove his beige Dodge on to the California State Fullerton campus, pulling into the parking lot on the west side of the library. He grabbed the rifle and ammunition, walking casually toward the library. Few people were in the library at the time, and he entered unnoticed. He took the stairwell to the basement and headed for the Instructional Media Center.

The Media Center was located adjacent to the stairwell. The secretary, Karen Dwinell, was just inside the door, sitting behind her desk. Thirty-year-old photographer Paul Herzberg was sitting on top of a table as he conversed with thirty-two-year-old, Bruce Jacobsen, an assistant at the media center. Allaway stepped into the office when Dwinell heard what she thought were firecrackers. Looking at Dwinell with a blank stare, Allaway raised his gun and pointed it at her.

Herzberg bolted toward Dwinell in an attempt to protect her when he felt himself getting shot in the chest. The second bullet entered his head. With a metal statue in his hand, Jacobson lunged toward Allaway, and he shot him in the chest. Despite being shot, Jacobson was able to run out of the office into the hall. As he ran away, Allaway stepped into the hall and shot Jacobsen a second time, killing him. Dwinell watched helplessly. She was also hit but survived her injuries.

Allaway continued down the hall and headed for the graphics department, also located in the basement. Seth Fessenden, professor emeritus, was discussing a project with fifty-year-old graphic artist, Frank Teplanksy. Allaway started firing immediately upon entering the department, shooting both men. Fessenden was killed instantly;

Teplansky died in the hospital several hours later, from a gunshot to the head.

Twenty-five-year-old Debbie Paulsen, a custodian at the university, also working on her Master's degree in American Studies, and a co-worker, forty-one-year-old Donald Karges, heard gunshots and went to investigate. As they headed down the hall, they saw Allaway at the other end. Recognizing the danger, they turned and ran, Allaway chasing after them.

Another secretary, Jenny Galvan, was sitting at her desk when she heard screams from the hall and footsteps of someone running. Looking through a small window in the door, she saw Paulsen collapse to the floor as if in slow motion. Galvan could see Paulsen had blood on her blouse and arms. She was gasping, and her eyes were barely open. She stopped moving. If Galvan had left her office, she would have seen Karges's body lying in a pool of blood further down the hall.

Richard Corona, the coordinator of the university's summer program known as Upward Bound, also heard the gunfire and went to investigate. As he turned the corner, Allaway rushed by him, making his way toward the stairwell. Allaway raised his gun to Corona, who was frozen on the spot. Allaway kept his gun pointed at Corona for a few seconds and then lowered it, choosing to run away instead.

Allaway reloaded in the stairwell and proceeded to the first floor. Sixty-four-year-old Maynard Hoffman, supervisor of the custodial crew for the morning shift, was walking down the hall on the first floor when Allaway appeared from the stairwell. Hoffman saw that he was armed and ran toward the elevator. As soon as the doors opened, he jumped inside. Before the elevator doors could close, Allaway emptied several rounds into it, with one bullet entering Hoffman's chest. He crumpled inside the bullet-ridden elevator.

Allaway stared down at him and asked him how it felt to be shot. Someone snuck up from behind Allaway and hit him over the head with a large earthenware plate. The plate shattered over Allaway's head, as a second person, thirty-two-year-old library technician, Steven Becker, attempted to wrestle Allaway's rifle from him.

As the struggle ensued, Becker was shot when the rifle went off. The wounded Becker ran away when library supervisor, fifty-one-year-old, Don Keran, appeared out of nowhere. He had heard the commotion and attempted to restrain Allaway in a bear hug.

Each man struggled to gain control of the other. Allaway pushed Keran against a wall, but Keran shoved him back. The pushing match continued until Keran fell backward. Allaway stood over him and pointed his rifle at him. When Keran struggled to get back on his feet, Allaway shot him.

As Allaway left the scene, Keran made it to a phone and called 911. He asked the 911 operator to send an ambulance and was told there were no ambulances available, as all ambulances had already been dispatched to the scene.

Allaway proceeded to run toward the emergency exit as Becker, though injured, gave chase. Allaway stopped in his tracks, turned around, and shot Becker a final time. Becker continued to struggle. He made it as far as the outside of the building, where he collapsed on the southeast side.

Keran and Hoffman both survived the attack; Becker, however, died en route to the hospital.

At the end of the five-minute rampage, seven people lost their lives, with another two suffering major injuries.

The Aftermath

Allaway got in his car and took off, eluding university police. He made his way to the Anaheim Hilton. After he was taken into custody, Fullerton police brought Allaway to the local jail. He was charged with six counts of first-degree murder, one count of second-degree murder, and two counts of assault with a deadly weapon.

At the end of his trial, he was ruled not guilty by reason of insanity and imprisoned at Atascadero State Hospital, then transferred to Patton State Hospital. Patton State Hospital was just fifty miles from the university.

Allaway's second wife filed for divorce shortly after the shooting.

Allaway's sister committed suicide by shooting herself.

Allaway was later transferred to Napa State Hospital, a low-security hospital, where he still resides. It was a move that was highly criticized. None of the victims' families had been consulted about the move.

The End of **The Preview**

Visit us at **truecrimeseven.com** or scan QR Code using your phone's **camera app** to find more true crime books and other cool goodies.

 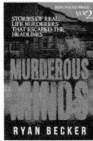  

 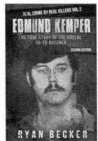  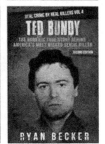

About True Crime Seven

True Crime Seven is about exploring the stories of the sinful minds in this world. From unknown murderers to well-known serial killers. It is our goal to create a place for true crime enthusiasts to satisfy their morbid curiosities while sparking new ones.

Our writers come from all walks of life but with one thing in common, and that is they are all true crime enthusiasts. You can learn more about them below:

Ryan Becker is a True Crime author who started his writing journey in late 2016. Like most of you, he loves to explore the process of how individuals turn their darkest fantasies into a reality. Ryan has always had a passion for storytelling. So, writing is the best output for him to combine his fascination with psychology and true crime. It is Ryan's goal for his readers to experience the full immersion with the dark reality of the world, just like how he used to in his younger days.

Nancy Alyssa Veysey is a writer and author of true crime books, including the bestselling, Mary Flora Bell: The Horrific True Story Behind an Innocent Girl Serial Killer. Her medical degree and work in the field of forensic psychology, along with postgraduate studies in criminal justice, criminology, and pre-law, allow her to bring a unique perspective to her writing.

Kurtis-Giles Veysey is a young writer who began his writing career in the fantasy genre. In late 2018, he parlayed his love and knowledge of history into writing nonfiction accounts of true crime stories that occurred in centuries past. Told from a historical perspective, Kurtis-Giles brings these victims and their killers back to life with vivid descriptions of these heinous crimes.

Kelly Gaines is a writer from Philadelphia. Her passion for storytelling began in childhood and carried into her college career. She received a B.A. in English from Saint Joseph's University in 2016, with a concentration in Writing Studies. Now part of the real world, Kelly enjoys comic books, history documentaries, and a good scary story. In her true-crime work, Kelly focuses on the motivations of the killers and backgrounds of the victims to draw a complete picture of each individual. She deeply enjoys writing for True Crime Seven and looks forward to bringing more spine-tingling tales to readers.

James Parker, the pen-name of a young writer from New Jersey, who started his writing journey with play-writing. He has always been fascinated with the psychology of murderers and how the media might play a role in their creation. James loves to constantly test out new styles and ideas in his writing so one day he can find something cool and unique to himself.

Brenda Brown is a writer and an illustrator-cartoonist. Her art can be found in books distributed both nationally and internationally. She has also written many books related to her graduate degree in psychology and her minor in history. Like many true crime enthusiasts, she loves exploring the minds of those who see the world as a playground for expressing the darker side of themselves—the side that people usually locked up and hid from scrutiny.

Genoveva Ortiz is a Los Angeles-based writer who began her career writing scary stories while still in college. After receiving a B.A. in English in 2018, she shifted her focus to nonfiction and the real-life horrors of crime and unsolved mysteries. Together with True Crime Seven, she is excited to further explore the world of true crime through a social justice perspective.

You can learn more about us and our writers at

https://truecrimeseven.com/about/

For updates about new releases, as well as exclusive promotions, join True Crime Seven readers' group and you can also **receive a free book today.** Thank you and see you soon.
Sign up at: **freebook.truecrimeseven.com/**

Or **scan QR Code using your phone's camera app.**

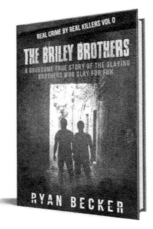

Dark Fantasies Turned Reality

Prepare yourself, we're not going to **hold back on details or cut out any of the gruesome truths...**

Made in the USA
Middletown, DE
05 May 2021